This is not our world with trees
in it. It's a world of trees, where
humans have just arrived.
—Richard Powers, *The Overstory*

For us all.
May peace and hope grow from
the darkest of our days.

—*MC & AB*

L B

LITTLE, BROWN AND COMPANY
New York   Boston

SURVIVOR TREE

WRITTEN BY

Marcie Colleen

ILLUSTRATED BY

Aaron Becker

A TREE STOOD STEEL-STRAIGHT AND PROUD
at the foot of the towers that filled its sky.

It grew, mostly unnoticed,
silently marking the seasons.

In wintertime, the tree's bare bones stretched tall,
reaching for the freezing bright blue above.

Come spring, white flowers blossomed.
Piles of petals scattered as people rushed by.

Glossy green leaves announced the arrival of summer,
casting polka-dotted shade on the sidewalk.

In fall, the tree blazed red with a million hearts
before each took off in an elegant dance.

And so it went for almost thirty years.

Winter, spring, summer, fall.
Bare, white, green, red.
Winter, spring, summer...

Fall.

One September day,
the perfect blue sky exploded.

Under the blackened remains,
the tree lay crushed and burned.

Workers dug through the wreckage
and discovered unexpected green.

The tree was taken far from the
smoldering landscape to fresh soil,
where its shattered stump encountered a different sky.

Two stone blocks were placed in its stunted shadow—
a memorial of makeshift towers in a makeshift home.
No longer stretching tall,
the tree reached deep in the warm earth,

and all was quiet.

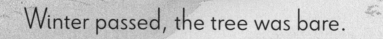

Winter passed, the tree was bare.

Spring arrived, without flowers,
but a flutter of speckled wings.

Then one day…
Buds to blossoms.
Blossoms to leaves.
Though charred and gnarled,
the tree began to grow.

And so it went
for almost ten years.

White, green, red, bare.
Spring, summer, fall...

Winter.

It was time to go home.

The
tree
hesitated
to
fill
the
empty
sky.

People no longer rushed by.
Instead, they stopped and wept
beside two forever-filling pools.

And they noticed the tree.

Fingers traced the timeline.

Warm palms pressed the old wound,
the bark joining the past to the present.

Today, the tree rises steel-straight and proud,
beside the footprints of the towers that once filled its sky.
Silently marking the seasons,
blazing with a million red hearts in the fall.

Our Survivor Tree.

THE SURVIVOR TREE

In October 2001, recovery workers discovered the remains of a Callery pear tree buried deep in the rubble of the World Trade Center. Its roots were severed, its crown was gone, its branches were burnt. Nonetheless, a bit of unseasonable green growth signaled that the tree was alive, but in distress. It soon became known as the last living thing pulled from the rubble.

The tree was placed in the care of the New York City Department of Parks & Recreation and replanted in the Arthur Ross Nursery in the Bronx on November 11, 2001. Its chances of survival were slim. The team at the nursery built a memorial around the tree, including two stone blocks to represent the fallen towers. Even with specialist care, the tree did not blossom, as hoped, in the spring. However, the story goes that soon after a dove nested in the tree's barren branches, buds began to appear.

For several years, the tree underwent a process of healing and rehabilitation. In December 2010, it was replanted as part of the 9/11 Memorial, where it provides a living timeline of the events of that tragic day. The rough bark of its trunk and lower branches symbolizes life before; a visible line of demarcation indicates the day the towers came down; and smooth new branches signify life after. Since its return, the tree has flourished and is often the first to bloom in the Memorial Plaza each spring.

The Survivor Tree seedling program started on September 11, 2013, in partnership with Bartlett Tree Experts of Stamford, Connecticut, and John Bowne High School in the Flushing neighborhood of Queens. Each year, seedlings from the Survivor Tree are given to three communities that have endured tragedy in recent years, so that they might plant their own symbol of a hopeful future.

AUTHOR'S NOTE

I was a teacher on September 11, 2001. As the day's events unfolded on our classroom television, I was asked countless questions by thirty-five high schoolers. My only answer: "I don't know." The blue early-morning sky had turned into a violent absence of color as gray ash brutally blotted out Lower Manhattan—a shift that haunted me long after the event, as did the many questions that I couldn't answer. It felt as if color might never return.

Then I learned of the 9/11 Survivor Tree.

The deeper I researched, the more I was struck by the Callery pear tree's brilliant seasonal display: white blossoms in spring, green leaves in summer, red leaves in autumn, and bare branches in winter—always with the promise that each color *will* reappear, in time. To tell this story of hope and healing, I could think of no better way than through the cycle of nature's seasons.

I was also amazed by the fact that the Callery pear tree species is predisposed to a short life, often topping out at twenty years. The Survivor Tree, planted at the base of the twin towers, had already lived a full life when it was crushed beneath twisted and tangled steel. Yet it survived. Those of us who remember that day all felt the world crashing down on us, too. Yet we survived. And color returned.

Shortly after completing this manuscript, I visited the tree at the 9/11 Memorial and quietly read the text aloud. When I was finished, I placed my palm on the tree's coarsely scarred bark and whispered, "I will tell your story." In doing so, I hope readers and their caregivers will find an entry point to a topic that is difficult to comprehend. I still do not have all the answers to the questions my students asked twenty years ago. But this book is what I can give them, and anyone seeking a more hopeful, colorful world.

—*Marcie Colleen*

The real Survivor Tree in 2018

ARTIST'S NOTE

The day after I visited the 9/11 Memorial & Museum to research the illustrations for this book, I'd planned a leisurely morning of bagel noshing before catching my train back home to Massachusetts. My sketchbook was full of notes, my camera full of pictures, and my imagination full of ideas. But there was still something missing.

So instead of my slow breakfast, I rushed to the uptown 4 subway train. By seven thirty, I was in the Bronx, heading toward a park I'd only learned of the day before. Arriving unannounced, I walked through a tall fenced gate and into the Arthur Ross Nursery, where for nearly ten years the Survivor Tree grew. I felt compelled to see the tree's second home, where it had been cared for, where it had sprouted new roots, where it had survived. The tree was gone now, having found a new home back at the memorial. But its seedlings grew in proud rows, their spring buds just beginning to flower in the cool, forested park. Life was everywhere.

When it came time to sketch out the story of the tree, details from my early-morning trip found their way into my drawings. But the nursery had also offered something less tangible for my artwork: hope. So I created a second story in the illustrations, one that crosses generations. Perhaps, like the tree, it will show readers that even in the darkest times, life will find its way.

Special thanks to Richard Cabo and the staff of the Arthur Ross Nursery for sharing their time and stories.

—*Aaron Becker*